Good Question!

Why Is the Sea Salty?
AND OTHER QUESTIONS ABOUT . . .
Oceans

STERLING CHILDREN'S BOOKS
New York

STERLING CHILDREN'S BOOKS
New York

An Imprint of Sterling Publishing
387 Park Avenue South
New York, NY 10016

Text © 2014 by Benjamin Richmond
Illustrations © 2014 Sterling Publishing Co., Inc.

Photo Credits: 4: Reto Stöckli, Nazmi El Saleous, and Marit Jentoft-Nilsen/NASA; 15: © Sean Pavone/Shutterstock; 19: © ifish/iStockphoto; © Rich Carey/Shutterstock

ISBN 978-1-4549-0676-6 [hardcover]
ISBN 978-1-4549-0677-3 [paperback]

Distributed in Canada by Sterling Publishing
c/o Canadian Manda Group, 165 Dufferin Street
Toronto, Ontario, Canada M6K 3H6
Distributed in the United Kingdom by GMC Distribution Services
Castle Place, 166 High Street, Lewes, East Sussex, England BN7 1XU
Distributed in Australia by Capricorn Link (Australia) Pty. Ltd.
P.O. Box 704, Windsor, NSW 2756, Australia

Design by Andrea Miller
Paintings by Cecelia Azhderian

For information about custom editions, special sales, and premium and corporate purchases, please contact Sterling Special Sales at 800-805-5489 or specialsales@sterlingpublishing.com.

Manufactured in China
Lot #:
2 4 6 8 10 9 7 5 3 1
04/14

www.sterlingpublishing.com/kids

CONTENTS

How much of Earth is covered with water?

When astronauts first looked at Earth from a distance, they described it as a "blue marble." That's because all the water on our planet makes it look blue. Although ice has been found on other planets and moons, Earth is the only planet that we know with liquid water. It is an incredible substance. Water can change from a solid to a liquid to a gas naturally on Earth. Without water, life as we know it could not exist. When scientists search the stars for planets that might have life, the key ingredient they look for is water.

Even though we call it "Earth," land covers only a small part of our planet. More than 70 percent of Earth's surface is water. If all dry land on Earth was pushed together, it would fit in the Pacific Ocean. The oceans cover 139 million square miles (mi^2), or 360 million square kilometers (km^2), of Earth's surface. That's about 67 billion football fields—a number that's hard to imagine.

Water is found everywhere on Earth. Some water is in rivers and lakes—some is even floating in the air as a gas called water vapor. Water is in clouds, underground, and even in your body—but most of Earth's water, over 96 percent, is found in the oceans.

What is an ocean?

An ocean is the biggest body of water on Earth. All of the world's oceans are connected. So, if you had a boat, you could sail through each of them. You probably wouldn't even notice crossing from one ocean to another. Because the same water flows between all of the oceans, many scientists think of them as just one big "world ocean."

To make it easier to map the planet, though, we talk about the world ocean as being five separate oceans: the Pacific Ocean, the Atlantic Ocean, the Indian Ocean, the Arctic Ocean, and the Antarctic, or Southern, Ocean. The seven biggest areas of land, called continents, help divide the world ocean. When an area of the ocean is partially surrounded by land, it is sometimes called a sea. Can you see the seas?

Be careful with the Caspian Sea in Asia! Although it is called a sea, the Caspian Sea doesn't connect to the ocean at all. And the water in the Caspian Sea is not as salty as the ocean. It might actually be the world's largest lake!

Even though the same water flows through all the oceans, the water changes as it moves. In the deeper parts of the ocean, the water becomes very cold. In parts of the Southern Ocean near Antarctica, and under the sea ice of the Arctic Ocean near the North Pole, temperatures can fall as low as 32 to 37 degrees Fahrenheit (°F), or 0 to 3 degrees Celsius (°C). But in the shallow parts of the ocean, like in the Gulf of Mexico, the water is warmed by the sun. Temperatures can rise to almost 90°F (32°C). That is nearly as warm as bathwater. The Indian Ocean is the warmest ocean, with an average temperature between 72 and 82°F (22–28°C). The Arctic Ocean is the coldest, with water usually right at freezing: 32°F (0°C). Sometimes the Arctic Ocean can be even colder than the temperature where water usually freezes. That's because the salt in the ocean lowers the freezing point.

The Water Cycle

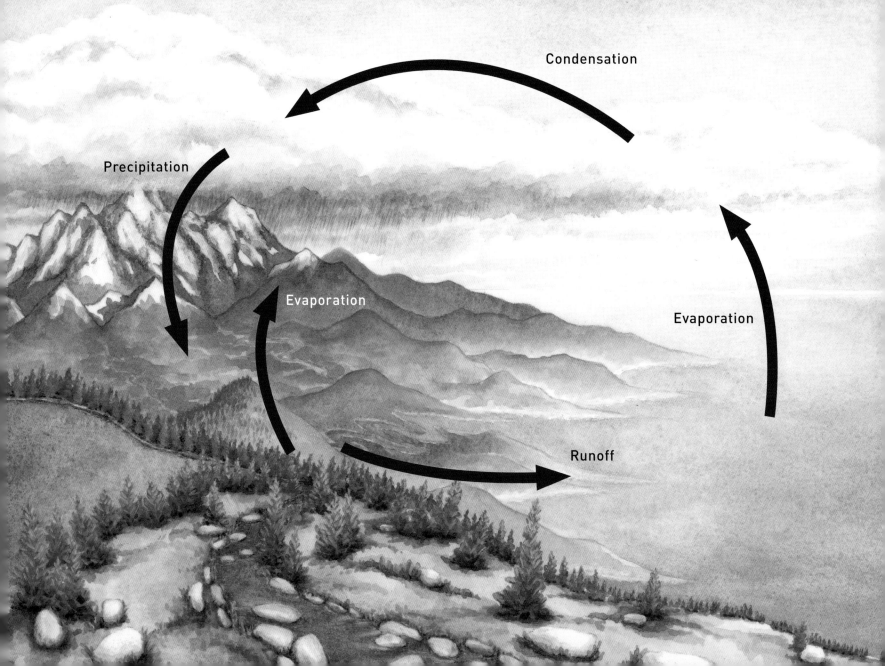

Condensation

Precipitation

Evaporation

Evaporation

Runoff

How does water get to the ocean?

Have you ever seen water trickle down a driveway and pool together in a puddle after a rainstorm? That's similar to how water travels to the ocean. Water makes its long journey to the ocean through a process called the water cycle. The water cycle is powered by the sun. Heat from the sun causes water to evaporate out of the ocean or lakes, changing it from a liquid into a gas called water vapor. Next, the water vapor floats up into the sky. When the water vapor starts to cool, it condenses, or collects, forming clouds. Eventually clouds get heavy with the condensing water vapor, and water droplets start to form. When they are too heavy to float, they precipitate, falling to Earth as rain or snow.

Some of the rain falls to the ground where thirsty plants use it to grow. Rain also collects into lakes and rivers, where animals can drink it. Water in rivers makes its way to the ocean, where it collects. Then, on a hot, sunny day, some water evaporates again and the water cycle starts over.

Why is the sea salty?

As rivers flow, they wear away at surrounding rocks and soil in a process called erosion. These tiny bits of rock, dirt, and minerals like salt are called sediment and are carried out to the ocean. Once in the ocean, sediment has nowhere else to go. Even when some of the water evaporates as part of the water cycle, the sediment gets left behind. The salt and other minerals build up and make the ocean salty. Over time, erosion can make big changes to the land and ocean. Over millions of years, the Colorado River actually carved out the Grand Canyon through erosion. It took millions of years of water flowing into the ocean for it to become as salty as it is today.

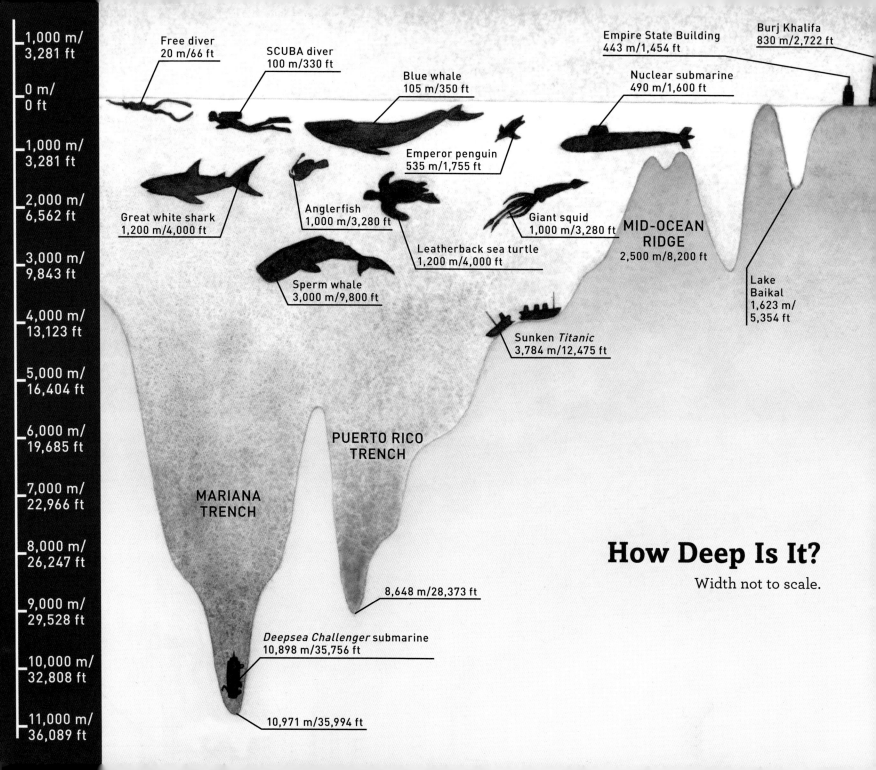

How Deep Is It?
Width not to scale.

How deep is the ocean?

I f you've ever walked into the ocean from the beach, you know that the ocean's depth changes a lot. The deepest point is in the Mariana Trench, located in the Pacific Ocean between Japan and Papua New Guinea. The deepest part of the trench, called the *Challenger Deep*, is 6.8 miles, or 11 kilometers (km), below the surface of the ocean. That is as far down as airplanes fly up in the sky. It is deep enough to bury Mount Everest, the world's tallest mountain, with plenty of room to spare. It is the lowest point on Earth.

But the ocean is shallow in some places, as in the Gulf of Mexico. Around the edges of the continents, the ocean is usually not as deep as it is farther from the shore. This edge is called the continental shelf. As you move away from the continental shelf, the ocean usually gets deeper. Sometimes this happens quickly, like the slope down a very steep hill.

Overall, the Pacific Ocean is the deepest ocean. Its average depth is 13,215 feet (ft), or 4,028 meters (m). The Arctic Ocean is the shallowest. Its average depth is 3,240 feet (987 m).

People used to think that the ocean floor was flat and bare, like a desert, but we now know the ocean floor is much more interesting. Not only is there a lot of life on the ocean floor, but there are also volcanoes and mountain ranges at the bottom of the ocean. In fact, the world's longest mountain range is actually underwater! It is called the mid-ocean ridge and it is 40,389 miles (65,000 km) long! The country of Iceland, which is an island, is actually the peak of one of these mountains.

What are the ocean zones?

You can divide the ocean into four different zones according to depth. Think of it like a layered cake. The top layer of the ocean is called the sunlit zone. This is where most sea creatures like dolphins, turtles, and the majority of fish live. The water is warmer here and there is plenty of food for these creatures to eat. Many kinds of plants and algae, like seaweed, live in the ocean, and almost all of them are found in the sunlit zone. This is because they need sunlight to grow.

Deeper in the ocean, past 660 feet (200 m), the light of the sun is barely visible. This zone is called the twilight zone. Twilight is the time of day right after the sun goes down but when some of its light is still lingering in the sky. The twilight zone is colder than the surface and there is not enough light for plants to grow. Swordfish, squid, wolf eels, and cuttlefish live in the twilight zone.

Even deeper still is the midnight zone. No sunlight can reach deeper than about 3,300 feet (1,000 m). It is always pitch black in the midnight zone, even in the middle of the day. The water here is very cold. Not many animals live in the midnight zone, but those that do live there don't use their eyes to find food. They use feelers and long hairs to sense ripples in the water. Tripod fish perch on their back fins on the ocean floor and hold out their front fins. When shrimp or tiny fish bump into a tripod fish's front fins, it scoops them into its mouth.

The deepest part of the ocean, like the Mariana Trench, is called the abyssal zone. At the bottom of the ocean, millions of gallons of water press down, causing a lot of pressure. There is life down in the abyssal zone, but it is very rare and usually very small.

SUNLIT ZONE

1. Plankton
2. Common cuttlefish
3. Blue whale
4. Great white shark
5. Bottlenose dolphin
6. Green sea turtle
7. Barracuda
8. Jack mackerel
9. Harbor seal
10. Dugong
11. Hammerhead shark
12. Clownfish
13. Clam

TWILIGHT ZONE

14. Oarfish
15. Longfin inshore squid
16. Hatchetfish
17. Northern elephant seal
18. Lanternfish
19. Coelacanth
20. Swordfish
21. Sperm whale
22. Barreleye fish
23. Comb jelly

MIDNIGHT ZONE

24. Sleeper shark
25. Scotoplanes (sea pig)
26. Anglerfish
27. Vampire squid
28. Gulper eel
29. Opossum shrimp
30. Cookiecutter shark

ABYSSAL ZONE

31. Abyssal snailfish
32. Tripod fish
33. Amphipod
34. Giant tube worm

NLIT
NE
560 ft
200 m

WILIGHT
NE
0–3,300 ft
0–1,000 m

ONIGHT
NE
00–13,100 ft
00–4,000 m

YSSAL
NE
,100+ ft
00+ m

What lives in the ocean?

From tiny plankton to the massive blue whale and from kelp to the Great Barrier Reef, the ocean is one of the most diverse habitats in the world. A habitat is where an animal or plant lives. There are many kinds of habitats, and each one is shared by different creatures and plants.

Almost every class of animal lives in the ocean. There are reptiles, like the sea turtle; mollusks, like oysters and clams; and arthropods, which include crabs and lobsters. Even mammals (the group that humans belong to) are represented by whales and dolphins.

Some animals in a habitat eat other animals. The hunters are called predators and the hunted animals are called prey. In the ocean, salmon eat smaller fish like herring, making the salmon predators. But salmon are eaten by seals, making the salmon prey. It's possible to be both prey and predator. Herring, salmon, and seals make up part of a food chain. Food chains can be very fragile. If all the herring were gone, the salmon would no longer have anything to eat and they could die. And that would cause the seals to have no food. This is why we have to be careful about overfishing the ocean. If we take out too many fish, the food chain could break and many animals would be in danger. They could even go extinct.

Can anything live at the bottom of the sea?

Some very strange animals live at the bottom of the sea. The Japanese spider crab can grow legs that span 13 feet (4 m)! Deep-sea isopods are related to pill bugs that you might see in the garden, but they can grow to over 1 foot (0.3 m) long and weigh more than 3 pounds, or 1 kilogram (kg).

In the deepest, darkest parts of the ocean, some fish make their own light, like fireflies do on land. The anglerfish goes "fishing" by using a glowing lure, and when a fish gets too close it snaps at its prey.

The Japanese spider crab is the world's biggest crab. And it can live up to 100 years!

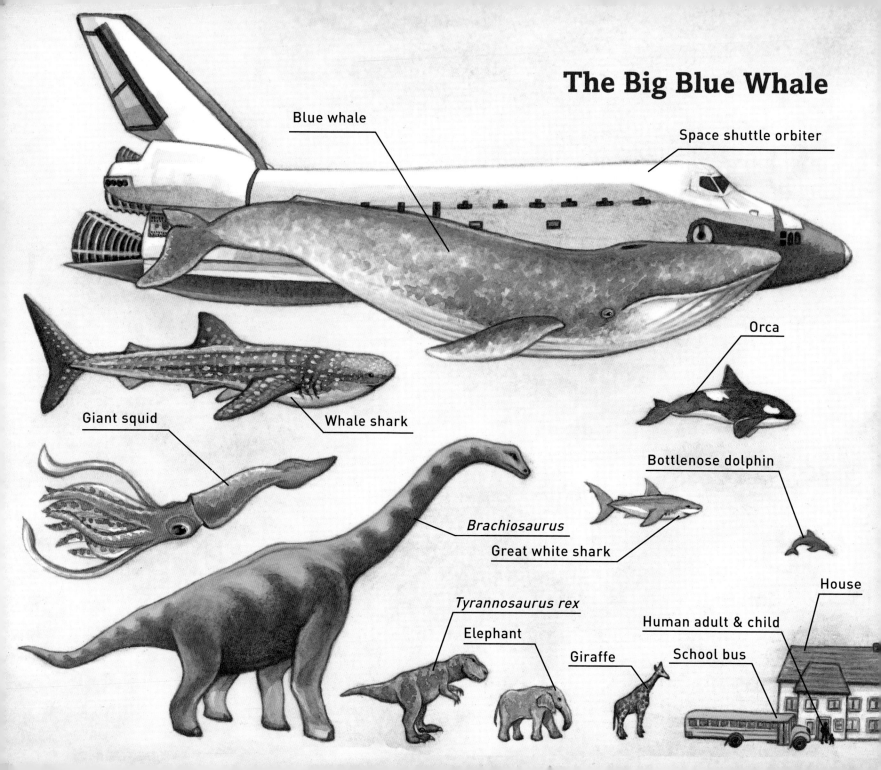

The Big Blue Whale

Blue whale

Space shuttle orbiter

Orca

Giant squid

Whale shark

Brachiosaurus

Bottlenose dolphin

Great white shark

House

Tyrannosaurus rex

Human adult & child

Elephant

Giraffe

School bus

What's the biggest animal in the ocean?

The biggest animal that has ever lived on Earth lives in the ocean right now. Bigger than any dinosaur, the blue whale is two and a half school buses long and weighs more than 200 tons (181,000 kg). Baby whales can gain 200 pounds (91 kg) in a single day. The tongue of an adult whale can be as heavy as an elephant, and its heart can be the size of a car! Blue whales are also some of the loudest creatures on Earth. They make pulsing sounds, groans, and clicks that can be heard by other whales a thousand miles away.

You might think an animal this big would have to eat other big creatures. But blue whales only eat krill, tiny relatives of shrimp that live in big groups in the open ocean. An adult blue whale eats 4 tons (3,629 kg) of krill every day. That's 8,000 pounds of krill!

What other large animals are out there?

The mysterious giant squid darts through the ocean's depths with two fins, eight legs, and two long tentacles. Giant squids have some of the biggest eyes in the animal kingdom, about as big as soccer balls—and they use them to see in the dim light of the deep ocean. They use suckers on their tentacles to snare fish and draw them to their beak-like mouths.

Giant squid can be 43 feet (13 m) in length. But for a long time, no one had ever seen an adult giant squid living in the wild. We only knew they existed because sometimes large tentacles from dead giant squid washed up on beaches or were found in the stomachs of sperm whales. In 2012, though, a live giant squid was filmed almost 3,000 feet (900 m) below the surface. Who knows what other creatures might be lurking in the deep that we haven't even discovered yet!

What's "the rainforest of the sea"?

Just like a rainforest, a coral reef is the heart of a very special kind of ecosystem, or group of plants and animals living together. Coral reefs form in warm, shallow water in the tropical parts of the world. A reef is actually made up of many different corals. While coral reefs can be very big, the animals that build them are actually tiny creatures called polyps, which are smaller than a quarter. They build protective skeletons around themselves out of a substance called calcium carbonate. They live together in colonies that over time become coral reefs. The biggest coral reef system is the Great Barrier Reef off the coast of Australia. At 1,600 miles (2,575 km) long, it's so big it can be seen from outer space.

Some animals live together in a coral reef and help each other. Many of these creatures have to get along in order to survive. The cleaner shrimp eats old food out of the moray eel's mouth, almost like a dentist cleans your teeth. The eel likes this, so it doesn't eat the cleaner shrimp. To avoid being eaten by bigger fish, the clown fish hides in the sea anemone, which looks like a flower or a mushroom, but instead of having petals, the sea anemone has poisonous tentacles. The clown fish has a coat of slime that protects it from the sea anemone. Some animals hide from predators in the coral reef, but some sneaky predators lurk there, too!

While coral reefs grow best in shallow, warm water, if the ocean gets too warm, the reefs will have trouble growing. All of the animals that live in the habitat need the reefs to survive, so it is important to protect them.

Coral reefs are home to nearly 25 percent of all ocean life.

How did rubber duckies help ocean scientists?

Just like water swirling down a drain, water moves in the ocean in great big circles. But what path does it follow? Scientists found answers from an unlikely source.

During a storm in 1992, a big container fell off a ship crossing the Pacific Ocean. When rubber duckies began washing to shore as far apart as Alaska and Oregon, it became clear that the container had been full of floating bathtub toys. When scientists found out where the duckies came ashore, they learned more about how the ocean moved.

Oceanographers, which are scientists who study the ocean, tracked the duckies. We now know that water in the Pacific Ocean takes about three years to travel in a big round shape called a gyre. Since water flows from ocean to ocean, rubber duckies showed up in Australia and in South America. Nearly ten years later, duckies began showing up in the Atlantic Ocean on America's east coast and in the United Kingdom. Some of the rubber duckies even traveled through the Arctic Ocean near the North Pole.

Is there a plastic island in the ocean?

In the middle of a gyre is an area of slow-moving water. In the Atlantic Ocean, this is called the Sargasso Sea. This area is full of seaweed, called Sargassum, which forms a forest for sea turtles and fish to live in.

But other things collect in the middle of the gyre, too. In the Pacific Ocean, plastics and other garbage are clumping together. This big trash pile is called the Great Pacific Garbage Patch. There is also a growing garbage patch in the North Atlantic Ocean. Plastic bags and bottles, lost fishing nets, and other trash are horrible for ocean life. Sea creatures choke on the garbage because they think it's food. Some fish eat small pieces of plastic, and the food chain could lead it all the way back to you!

To fight the growing garbage patches, be sure not to leave trash on the beach. You could even collect and throw away garbage you find there to help keep the ocean clean.

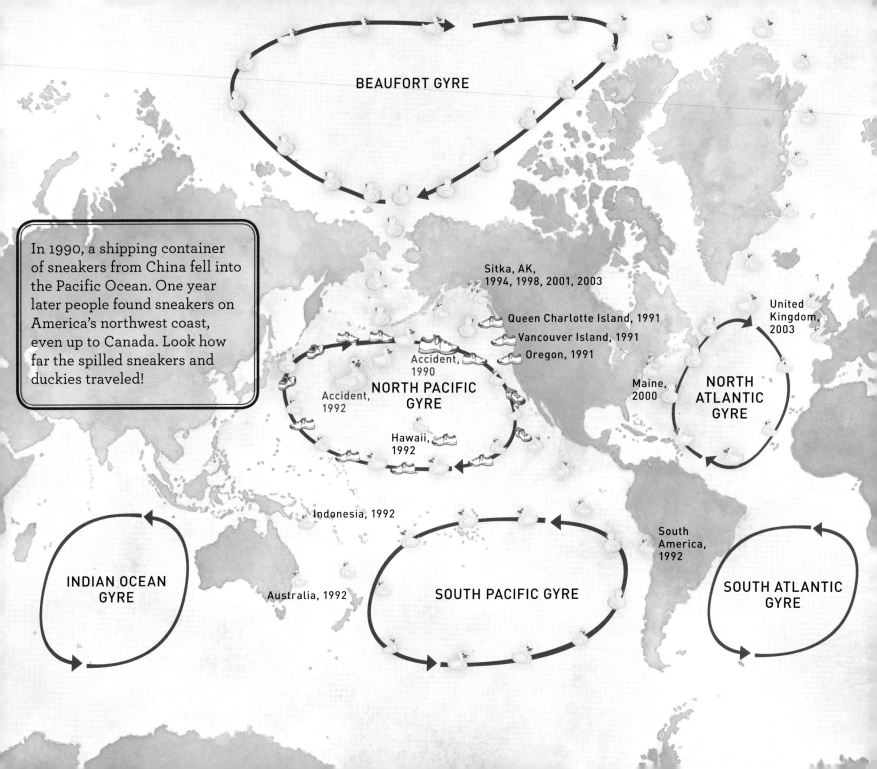

BEAUFORT GYRE

In 1990, a shipping container of sneakers from China fell into the Pacific Ocean. One year later people found sneakers on America's northwest coast, even up to Canada. Look how far the spilled sneakers and duckies traveled!

Sitka, AK,
1994, 1998, 2001, 2003

Queen Charlotte Island, 1991

Vancouver Island, 1991

Oregon, 1991

Accident,
1990

NORTH PACIFIC
GYRE

Accident,
1992

Hawaii,
1992

United Kingdom,
2003

Maine,
2000

NORTH ATLANTIC GYRE

Indonesia, 1992

South America,
1992

INDIAN OCEAN GYRE

Australia, 1992

SOUTH PACIFIC GYRE

SOUTH ATLANTIC GYRE

Does the ocean predict the weather?

Have you ever noticed that the weather near the ocean is different from the weather farther inland? This is because the ocean affects the weather. Think about England and Scotland. They are as far north as the middle of Canada, but the middle of Canada has much colder winters. This is because ocean currents bring warm water from the Gulf of Mexico up the east coast of America and then all the way over to England, heating the climate. When water moves in a definite direction, it is called a current.

Each ocean has currents that flow through it almost like rivers. Ocean currents bring hurricanes from the North Atlantic Ocean toward the Caribbean Sea. Currents also help people move across the ocean faster. Before boats had motors, currents helped sailors travel across the ocean.

What are the world's largest storms?

Hurricanes are the biggest storms on earth. Powered by warm water in the ocean, these disastrous storms follow ocean currents, bringing pounding wind and rain. They are so big that astronauts can see them from space. Hurricanes look like big clouds spinning like tops. They have a hole in the center called the eye of the storm. The fastest winds surround the eye, and they can reach 190 miles (306 km) per hour. But inside the eye, the wind is calm. Hurricanes can last for weeks and stretch for hundreds of miles. In 2012, Hurricane Sandy hit the east coast of the United States and brought giant waves to shore. The wind and water caused $50 billion worth of damage.

Hurricanes form over warm ocean water, usually warmer than 80°F (27°C). In the Atlantic Ocean, hurricane season lasts from June until the end of November. In the Pacific Ocean, hurricanes are called typhoons, and typhoon season starts in May and goes until the end of November. In the Indian Ocean, these kinds of storms are called cyclones. Hurricanes don't form over the Arctic and Antarctic Oceans because the water is too cold!

The North Atlantic Current keeps London's winters mild and also causes the city's famous fog.

In 2011, an underwater earthquake caused a huge 133-foot (40-m) tsunami that hit Japan and caused a lot of damage.

How does the moon move the oceans?

When you think of gravity, you might think of it as the force that pulls an apple down from a tree. And that's true. Gravity is what attracts, or pulls, two objects together. But did you know the moon's gravity is pulling things on Earth?

The scientist Isaac Newton discovered that everything with mass is pulled toward everything else with mass. Mass is the amount of matter, or stuff, that something is made of. Things with a lot of mass, like Earth or the moon, have a stronger pull than things without much mass, like an apple. The moon's pull, or gravity, is not strong enough to snatch an apple from a tree and bring it to the moon, but it is strong enough to move the ocean!

As the moon travels around Earth, it pulls on the ocean. Earth's gravity is much stronger than the moon's, so the ocean doesn't get sucked into space, but it does move. When the ocean is being pulled toward land, it rises and covers more, or all, of the beach. This is called high tide. Later, when the moon is on the other side of Earth, the ocean gets pulled out and the beach seems to grow. This is called low tide. Most places experience two high tides and two low tides a day.

What causes waves?

Surfers love to ride big, curling, crashing waves. Most waves are caused by the wind blowing across the surface of the water. Out at sea, the waves don't "break," or crash. Because they don't have a shore to break against, the water only rises up and then goes back down. A rising and falling wave is called a swell.

There are also big, sometimes dangerous, waves called tsunamis. A tsunami is caused by earthquakes or volcanic eruptions under the sea. When the ocean floor shifts, all the water is moved, too. This causes massive waves. To keep people safe, scientists use underwater earthquakes as warnings for tsunamis.

Will the ocean always stay the same?

The ocean is always changing, but sometimes it changes so slowly that we barely notice. Did you know the Atlantic Ocean is getting wider and the Pacific Ocean is shrinking? North and South America are drifting west, very, very slowly, moving only about 1 inch, or 2.5 centimeters every a year. The movement is so slow that scientists can track it with special equipment, but people do not notice the shift. But the ocean is also changing in other, less natural ways.

The plastic island in the ocean is an unnatural, man-made problem, but there is other pollution, too. Pesticides used on farms to protect plants from bugs can cause big problems for the ocean. When it rains, the pesticides can wash off and get into rivers that flow into the ocean. This can poison ocean life, killing the plants and animals that live there.

Another problem is Earth's rising temperature. When people burn oil, coal, or gasoline, it releases a gas called carbon dioxide, or CO_2. When too much carbon dioxide is in the air, it traps heat from the sun on Earth. This makes Earth warmer, little by little, each year. These little changes matter a lot. More and more ice in Antarctica and Greenland melts each year, and that water flows into the ocean, causing it to rise.

Does it matter if the ocean rises?

Yes! The rising ocean affects everyone, but especially the people who live close to the water. If the ocean rose 6 feet (2 m), the city of Amsterdam would flood. If the ocean rose 10 feet (3 m), San Francisco would flood. We are already seeing a slow rise in the ocean from global warming. If this continues, scientists believe the ice caps will melt and the ocean could rise more than 230 feet (70 m). This would flood the coasts, and at least 500 million people would have to leave their homes.

Melting ice caps are causing the oceans to rise.

How much do we know about the ocean?

Many different types of scientists focus on the ocean. Geologists study the ocean's many volcanoes and earthquakes, and they map the mountains and valleys on the ocean floor. Meteorologists study the weather as it travels across the ocean. Oceanographers study how the ocean moves. Marine biologists study the many things living in the ocean. And all of these scientists have so much more to learn!

Some people call the ocean floor the final frontier because it is even more mysterious than outer space or the surface of the moon. Twelve people have walked on the moon, but only three have been down to the Mariana Trench.

Some biologists are tracking animals like sea turtles and seals that make long journeys, traveling thousands of miles across the ocean. They use harmless tags attached to the animals that send information to scientists via satellite. Not only do researchers learn about where animals go and how fast they travel, but they can also gather information about the ocean water that these creatures are swimming in, like its temperature and depth.

There is still so much on the bottom of the ocean that we are just beginning to understand. Worms live down in the complete darkness of the ocean floor near volcanic vents. The vents shoot out hot gases, like steam out of a tea kettle, along with nutrients and minerals. Tiny bacteria, or creatures too small to see, live on those nutrients, and the worms eat those bacteria. It's a very unusual way to live, and scientists are excited to see what other ways life flourishes in the mysterious ocean.

Compare the Oceans

OCEAN	AREA	AVERAGE DEPTH	GREATEST DEPTH	BIGGEST ISLAND	BIGGEST CONNECTING SEA
Pacific	60,060,700 mi² (155,557,000 km²)	13,215 ft (4,028 m)	Mariana Trench 35,840 ft (10,924 m)	New Guinea	Philippine Sea
Atlantic	41,105,000 mi² (106,460,000 km²)	12,880 ft (3,926 m)	Puerto Rico Trench 28,231 ft (8,605 m)	Greenland (biggest island in the world)	Caribbean Sea
Indian	26,469,900 mi² (68,566,000 km²)	13,002 ft (3,963 m)	Java Trench 23,812 ft (7,258 m)	Madagascar	Arabian Sea
Southern	7,848,300 mi² (20,327,000 km²)	13,100 to 16,400 ft (4,000 to 5,000 m)	End of South Sandwich Trench 23,737 ft (7,235 m)	Alexander Island	Amundsen Sea
Arctic	5,427,000 mi² (14,056,000 km²)	3,953 ft (1,205 m)	Fram Basin 15,305 ft (4,665 m)	Greenland is also in the Arctic Ocean, but Baffin Island is the biggest island solely in the Arctic Ocean	Barents Sea

FIND OUT MORE

Books to Read

Curry, Don L. and Gail Saunders-Smith. *The Water Cycle*. Capstone, 2000.

Gray, Samantha. *Ocean*. Dorling Kindersley Publishing, 2001.

Johansson, Philip. *The Seashore: A Saltwater Web of Life*. Enslow Publishers, 2007.

Parker, Steve. *Ocean and Sea*. Scholastic, 2012.

Websites to Visit

MARINE BIOLOGY FACTS
http://marinebio.org/marinebio/facts/

NATIONAL GEOGRAPHIC OCEAN PAGE FOR KIDS
http://kids.nationalgeographic.com/kids/activities/new/ocean/

NATIONAL OCEANIC AND ATMOSPHERIC ADMINISTRATION PAGE FOR KIDS
http://oceanservice.noaa.gov/kids/

OCEANS FOR YOUTH FOUNDATION'S KID'S CORNER PAGE
www.oceansforyouth.org/kidscorner.html

For bibliography and free activities visit: http://www.sterlingpublishing.com/kids/good-question

INDEX